.

A WISCONSIN BIRD ALPHABET

Caitlynn Nemec

OrangeHat

Orange Hat Publishing
www.orangehatpublishing.com - Waukesha, WI

For information, please contact:

Orange Hat Publishing
www.orangehatpublishing.com

Cover design by Caitlynn Nemec and Shannon Ishizaki

The author has made every effort to ensure that the accuracy of the information within this book was correct at time of publication. The author does not assume and hereby disclaims any liability to any party for any loss, damage, or disruption caused by errors or omissions, whether such errors or omissions result from accident, negligence, or any other cause.

To Evelyn and Adeline.

May wild places always be
in your heart and in your life.

A

American Robin

Hopping through the grass eating worms in the spring,

Grey back, dark head, rusty tummy, white eye ring.

His tummy's quite round and his legs are long,

And a sure sign of spring is his cheerful song.

This singing thrush we are so happy to see,

"Cheer-up, cheer-e-o, cherr-a-lee!"

B

Bobolink

If in a grassy field you hear a robot or maybe a "plink,"

You will spy the little blackbird named Bobolink.

He has a yellow cap and a patchy white rump,

And sings a bubbly song building his nest in a clump.

In his backwards tuxedo he looks quite snappy.

Insects and grubs make him quite happy.

C

Cedar Waxwing

On cold, calm days if you can stand it,

You'll find a winter berry bandit.

Cedar waxwing you silky bird,

Your high pitched call can be heard,

Atop berry laden trees and things,

With your yellow tipped tail and waxy red tipped wings.

D

Dickcissel

This grassland bird may have a stutter when he says his name,

But with his fancy, flashy looks you cannot call him plain.

His bright yellow breast and trim black beard do not go amiss,

When he calls out his own name "D'-d'-dic-sis-sis-sis!"

He has a stout and pointy bill and a yellow eye stripe.

He enjoys an insect or two and seeds when they are ripe.

E

Eastern Meadowlark

In the grasslands can be found,

A handsome bird nesting on the ground.

With brown streaked above a bright yellow chest,

A long bill and a black "V" on his breast.

He proudly tips his head to sing,

Sounding like a squeaky old swing.

"Seeeoooaa-seeeadoo!"

F

Purple Finch

If you set out a feeder you may get lucky,

And see a little red bird that's a bit stocky.

He eats sunflower seeds or thistle in a sack,

Flashing a short, notched tail and reddish-brown back.

His songs are warbling, fast, lively, and brief,

Nesting in trees with needles or many a leaf.

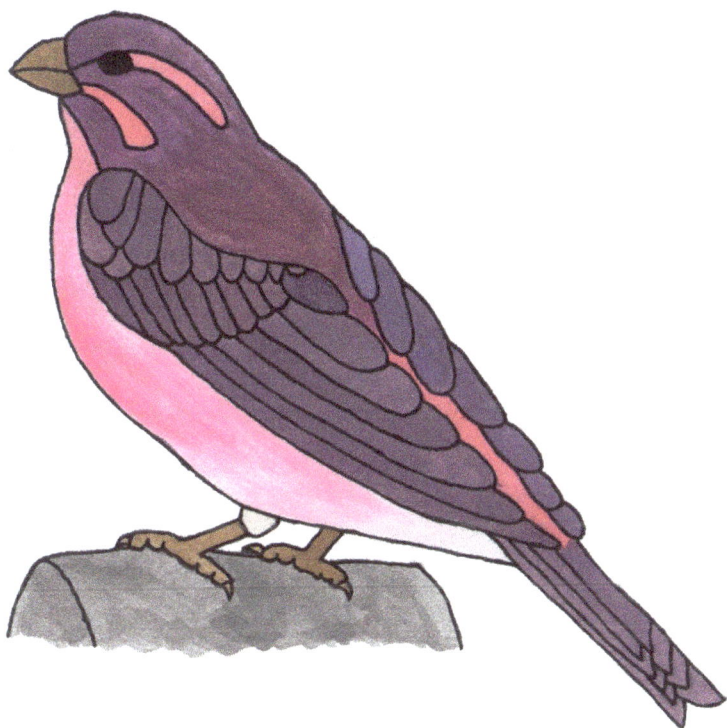

G

Greater Prairie Chicken

In the spring you'll need a compass,

To find the low hooting, clucking rumpus.

It is a show you must not miss,

Where lekking males hope for a kiss.

Watch drumming feet and orange sacks of air.

Their brown and tan ladies sure will be there!

H

Henslow's Sparrow

In weedy grasslands with sparse shrubs,

Lives a sparrow who eats insects and grubs.

He has a handsome, thick bill and large head,

Builds on the ground where he makes his mate's bed.

Showing off rufus wings and olive-green neck.

He sounds like a hiccup or maybe an insect.

"Ts-lick"

Indigo Bunting

From the tops of trees a little, blue bird,

Sings songs of warning to be heard.

"Fire! Fire! Where? Where?

Here! Here! See it? See it?"

He then searches trees for his needs

Of insects, grubs, berries, and seeds.

Or he may come by to have a snack,

At your thistle hanging in a sack.

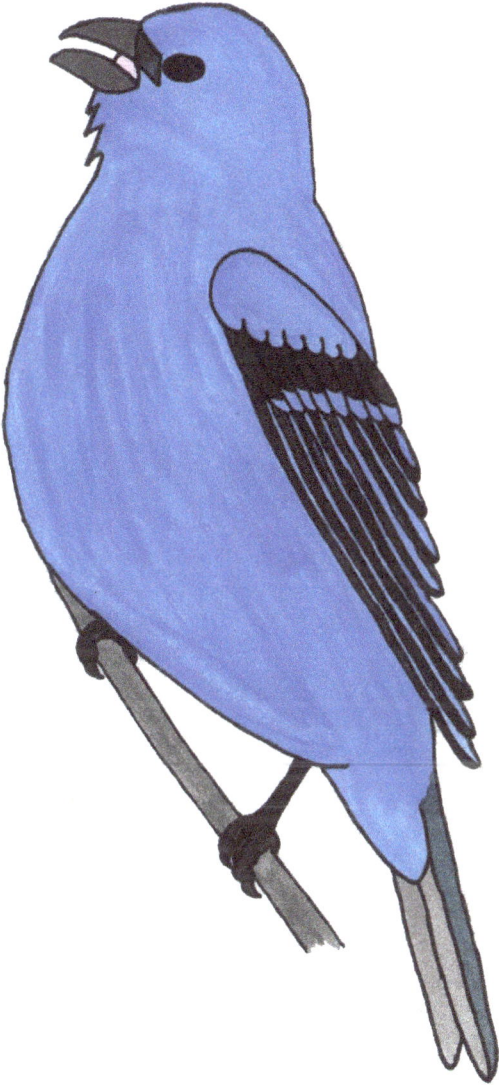

J

Blue Jay

If you go out to the woods where the trees are tall,

You'll find a big blue bird eating acorns in the fall.

He has black and white on his wings and gray below,

A fancy head crest and a long tail, don't you know?

He'll also enjoy some of your seeds any day,

And is noisy and flashy when he calls, "Jay! Jay! Jay!"

K

Kirtland's Warbler

This rare little bird is a rather picky fellow,

With blue-gray above and a belly of yellow.

He prefers young jack pine trees near his nest,

Because the insects he gleans off of them are the best.

He builds a sneaky little nest hidden on the ground,

And sings, "Chip, chip, che-way-o" flicking his tail up and down.

L

Least Bittern

Out in the marshes on the water's edge,

A tiny heron goes fishing by the cattails and sedge.

He can be hard to spot, standing still as he hunts.

Look for black backs and orange and white striped fronts.

If you can't spot his long bill and neck when it's light,

Listen for his long soft "wuff-wuff-wuff" at night.

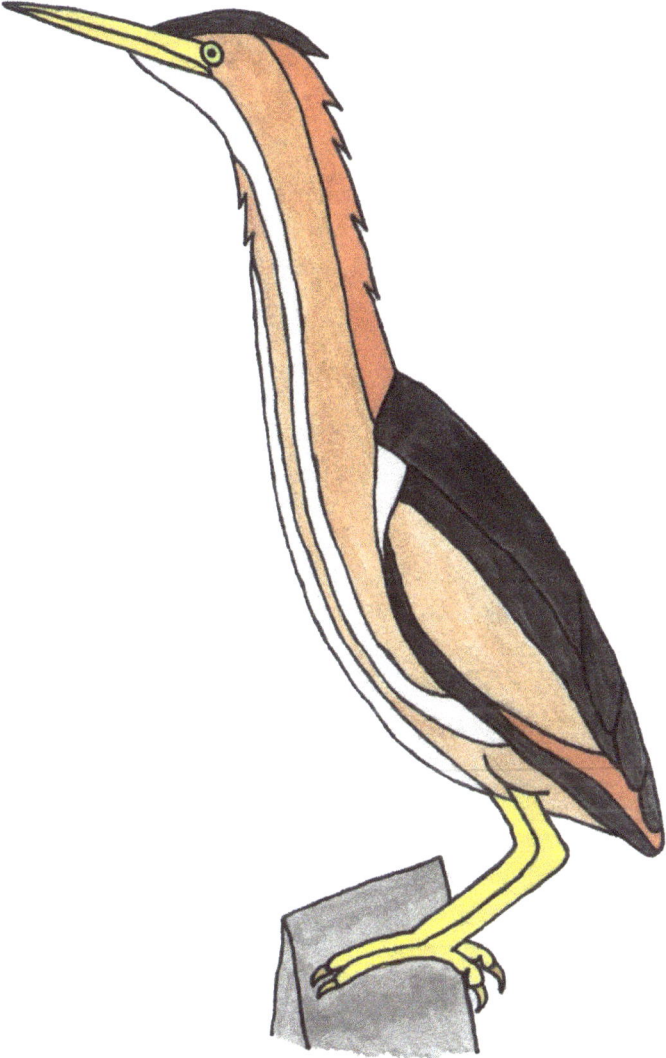

M

Mourning Dove

Outside your front door you may hear a call like an owl,

But it may in fact be a very different kind of fowl.

He has a brown chunky body, pointed tail, and small head,

Dark spots on his wings and a pinkish-beige belly to be fed.

You can see him search the lawn for seeds near you,

And hear his low haunting call "Hoo-ah, hoo, hoo, hoo."

N

Northern Harrier

Here we have a regal hawk, a true bird of prey,

Flying low over fields and marshes spending his day.

With his short beak, flat face, and tail held in a "V,"

He listens closely for his dinner to find what he can't see.

He's gray above and white below with black wing tips,

With a long tail and thin wings as he swoops and dips.

O

Barred Owl

Sometimes in the day where the trees are tall,

You'll hear an owl calling "Who cooks for you? Who cooks for you all?"

At night he's a hunter waiting quietly up above,

To catch the mammals, amphibians, and fish that he does love.

He has brown and white feathers and black eyes,

And makes not even a sound when he flies.

P

Pileated Woodpecker

If while deep in the woods you hear a drumming,

A big black bird with white neck stripes may be coming.

He has white under wings and flaming red atop his head,

And drills rectangular holes in trees to make his bed.

He chisels decayed trees with his long neck and powerful bill,

Flying from tree to tree looking for carpenter ants to get his fill.

Q

Northern Bobwhite Quail

This patterned brown bird may be hard to spot,

But if you listen in the brush in places he is sought,

You can hear him call his name very loud and clear.

So when you hear, "Bob-white" you know that he is near.

He'll hide his black and white face on the ground,

For that is where his seeds and leaves are to be found.

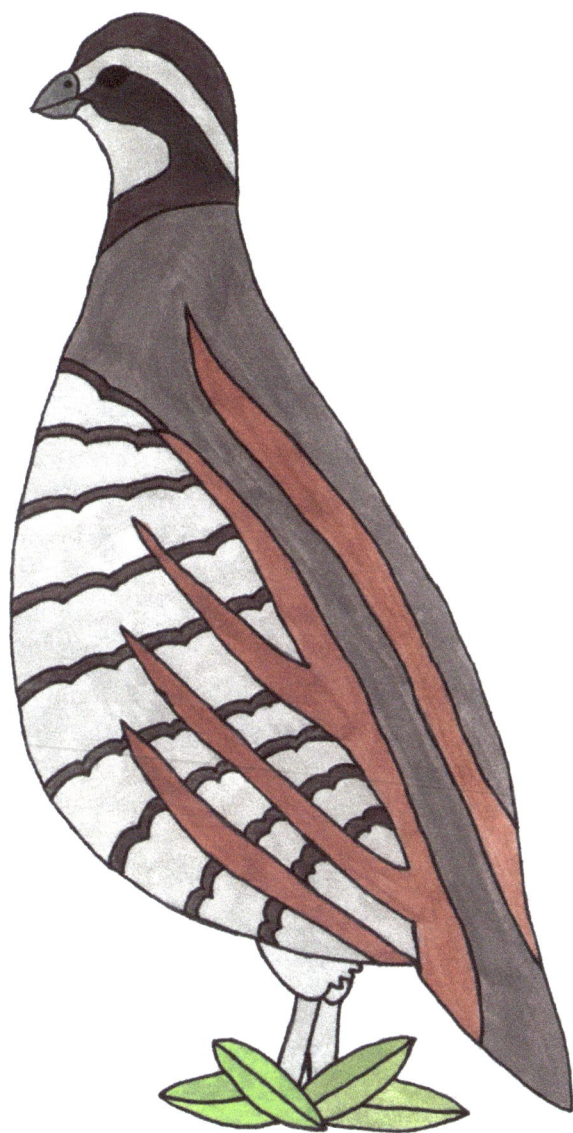

R

Ruby Throated Hummingbird

In the summer, be sure to plant lots of nectar flowers,

To bring a bird that darts and hovers just like it has magic powers.

He flaps his wings so mighty fast it sounds just like a plane,

With green above, white below, and a red chin just like a stain.

He'll also dip his down curved bill into a sugar feeder,

But look real fast or you'll miss him this green little speeder.

S

Sandhill Crane

A large bird roams the marshes in the summer.

His long legs, gray body, and red crown make him quite a stunner.

His bugling call can carry far and wide,

While he eats grains and bugs that cannot hide.

He courts his mate with a bowing leaping dance,

To build a grass nest on the ground if he gets his chance.

T

Tufted Titmouse

A little gray bird may visit the feeder that is in your yard,

Taking seeds back to his cache, cracking open shells that are hard.

He also enjoys insects from the trees near his nest,

That he builds in holes left by woodpeckers after their rest.

He has a small bill, gray crest, and large black eyes.

Listen as he calls, "Peter-peter-peter" at the sunrise.

U

Upland Sandpiper

Perched high up on a shrub or maybe a fence post,

Sits a brown and beige bird that likes prairies the most.

He has a small head, long neck, and large eye.

A long tailed, straight billed, tall legged guy.

When he gets up to fly you may hear his wolf whistle,

As he's off to find insects in the grass and the thistle.

V

Veery

If you hear a cascading song like a flute in a band,

You'll find a little cinnamon bird living in the woodland.

He has a plump, round, white belly and a buffy breast,

Round head, narrow bill, and washed out spots on his chest.

He likes to build his nest near the ground,

And looks for insects and fruit when it can be found.

W

White Breasted Nuthatch

Leave out some seeds or maybe some suet,

And a searching little bird may come to it.

He has a clean white face with a black cap.

He's a rusty bellied, blue-gray backed chap.

He cracks his seeds whacking them with his bill,

And if you listen quietly you may hear him still.

"Wha-wha-wha-wha-wha-wha-wha!"

X

Fox Sparrow

If you look below your bird feeder this winter,

You'll find a big sparrow kicking in the leaf litter.

He forages for seeds and insects on the ground,

Whistles richly and makes a puckering kiss sound.

He can be red like a fox or sometimes a bit brown,

A stout bill, streaky splotchy chest, and a gray crown.

Y

Yellow Bellied Sapsucker

If you come across a row of holes drilled deep into a tree,

A clever little woodpecker around you there must be.

He makes his holes to lick the sap and insects that come to it.

With his red cap and white shoulder stripe you may find him on your suet.

Even with his bold face stripes he may look a little frumpy.

Listen for his hole drilling that sounds stuttered and bumpy.

Z

Zebra Finch

Alas there is no native bird with a Z in his name.

This seems to be quite a sad end to our game.

But in many a home an exotic bird can be found,

That finishes our alphabet and brings it around.

The zebra finch sings a song so nice,

And you can have one in a cage for a small price.

www.ingramcontent.com/pod-product-compliance
Lightning Source LLC
Chambersburg PA
CBHW040805150426
42813CB00056B/2655